SRA
Reading Mastery
Signature Edition

Literature Anthology

Siegfried Engelmann
Susan Hanner

Columbus, OH

Acknowledgements

Grateful acknowledgement is given to the following publishers and copyright owners for permissions granted to reprint selections from their publications. All possible care has been taken to trace ownership and secure permission for each selection included. In case of any errors or omissions, the Publisher will be pleased to make suitable acknowledgements in future editions.

Annick Press

© STEPHANIE'S PONYTAIL, written by Robert Munsch and illustrated by Michael Martchenki. Published by Annick Press 1996.

Farrar, Straus and Giroux

THE THREE WISHES: AN OLD STORY by Margot Zemach. Copyright © 1986 by Margot Zemach. Reprinted by permission of Farrar, Strauss and Giroux, LLC.

Melissa Heckler

"A House with a Star Inside" Retold by Melissa A. Heckler. Used with permission of the author.

Pamela Mordecai

"Rabbit Poem" first published in A CARRIBEAN DOZEN: POEMS FROM CARRIBEAN POETS (Walker Books and Candlewick Press, 1990)

"Remember" first published in STORYPOEMS – A FIRST COLLECTION (Ginn & Co, 1987)

"Moonwalker", "Swap", from LUNCH MONEY by Carol Diggory Shields, copyright © 1995 by Carol Diggory Shields, text. Used by permission of Dutton Children's Books, A Division of Penguin Young Readers Group, A Member of Penguin Group (USA) Inc., 345 Hudson Street, New York, NY 10014. All rights reserved.

Thomson Learning Australia

TOM'S FRIEND by Pat Reynolds, TRIXIE by Rick Brownell, POP'S TRUCK by Sally George and GEORGE AT THE ZOO by Sally George used by permission of Thomson Learning Australia.

SRAonline.com

 SRA

Send all inquiries to this address:
SRA/McGraw-Hill
4400 Easton Commons
Columbus, OH 43219

ISBN: 978-0-07-612544-9
MHID: 0-07-612544-0

8 9 10 11 QWD 13 12 11 10 09

TABLE OF CONTENTS

TABLE OF CONTENTS
continued

Stephanie's Ponytail

Story by Robert Munsch

Art by Michael Martchenko

One day Stephanie went to her mom and said, "None of the kids in my class have a ponytail. I want a nice ponytail coming right out the back."

So Stephanie's mom gave her a nice ponytail coming right out the back.

When Stephanie went to school the other kids looked at her and said, "Ugly, ugly, *very* ugly."

Stephanie said, "It's *my ponytail* and *I* like it."

3

The next morning, when Stephanie went to school, all the other girls had ponytails coming out the back.

Stephanie looked at them and said, "You are all a bunch of copycats. You just do whatever I do. You don't have a brain in your heads."

The next morning the mom said, "Stephanie, would you like a ponytail coming out the back?"

Stephanie said, "No."

"Then that's that," said her mom. "That's the only place you can do ponytails."

"No, it's not," said Stephanie. "I want one coming out the side, just above my ear."

"Very strange," said the mom. "Are you sure that is what you want?"

"Yes," said Stephanie.

So her mom gave Stephanie a nice ponytail coming out right above her ear.

When she went to school the other kids saw and said, "Ugly, ugly, *very* ugly."

Stephanie said, "It's *my ponytail* and *I* like it."

The next morning when Stephanie came to school all the girls, and even some of the boys, had nice ponytails coming out just above their ears.

The next morning the mom said, "Stephanie, would you like a ponytail coming out the back?"

Stephanie said, "NNNO."

"Would you like one coming out the side?"

"NNNO!"

"Then that's that," said her mom. "There is no other place you can do ponytails."

"Yes, there is," said Stephanie. "I want one coming out the top of my head like a tree."

"That's very, very strange," said her mom. "Are you sure that is what you want?"

"Yes," said Stephanie.

So her mom gave Stephanie a nice ponytail coming out the top of her head like a tree. When Stephanie went to school, the other kids saw her and said, "Ugly, ugly, *very* ugly."

Stephanie said, "It's *my ponytail* and *I* like it."

The next day all of the girls and all of the boys had ponytails coming out the top. It looked like broccoli was growing out of their heads.

The next morning the mom said, "Stephanie, would you like a ponytail coming out the back?"

Stephanie said, "NNNO."

"Would you like one coming out the side?"

"NNNO!"

"Would you like one coming out the top?"

"NNNO!"

"Then that is definitely that," said the mom. "There is no other place you can do ponytails."

"Yes, there is," said Stephanie. "I want one coming out the front and hanging down in front of my nose."

"But nobody will know if you are coming or going," her mom said. "Are you sure that is what you want?"

"Yes," said Stephanie.

So her mom gave Stephanie a nice ponytail coming out the front.

On the way to school she bumped into four trees, three cars, two houses and one Principal. When she finally got to her class the other kids saw her and said, "Ugly, ugly, *very* ugly." Stephanie said, "It's *my ponytail* and *I* like it."

The next day all of the girls and all of the boys, and even the teacher, had ponytails coming out the front and hanging down in front of their noses. None of them could see where they were going. They bumped into the desks and they bumped into each other. They bumped into the walls, and, by mistake, three girls went into the boys' bathroom.

Stephanie yelled, "You are a bunch of brainless copycats. You just do whatever I do. When I come tomorrow I am going to have . . . SHAVED MY HEAD!"

The first person to come the next day was the teacher. She had shaved her head and she was bald.

The next to come were the boys. They had shaved their heads and they were bald.

The next to come were the girls. They had shaved their heads and they were bald.

The last person to come was Stephanie, and she had . . .

a nice little ponytail coming right out the back.

21

23

GEORGE AT THE ZOO

Written by Sally George
Illustrated by Rob Mancini

George was a small dog who liked large bones and going on picnics. So when his family got out the picnic basket, George got very excited.

"No, George!" said his family. "We're going to the zoo. Dogs can't go to the zoo."

But George liked going in the car, and
smelling new smells, and running in new
places, and, especially, eating the picnic.
So when his family wasn't looking,
George jumped inside the picnic basket.
The lid closed, and nobody saw him.

26

They picked up the picnic basket and carried it out to the car. It was very dark in the picnic basket. And very crowded.

There was more room after George ate the cold chicken, and the ham, and the rolls, and half the cake.

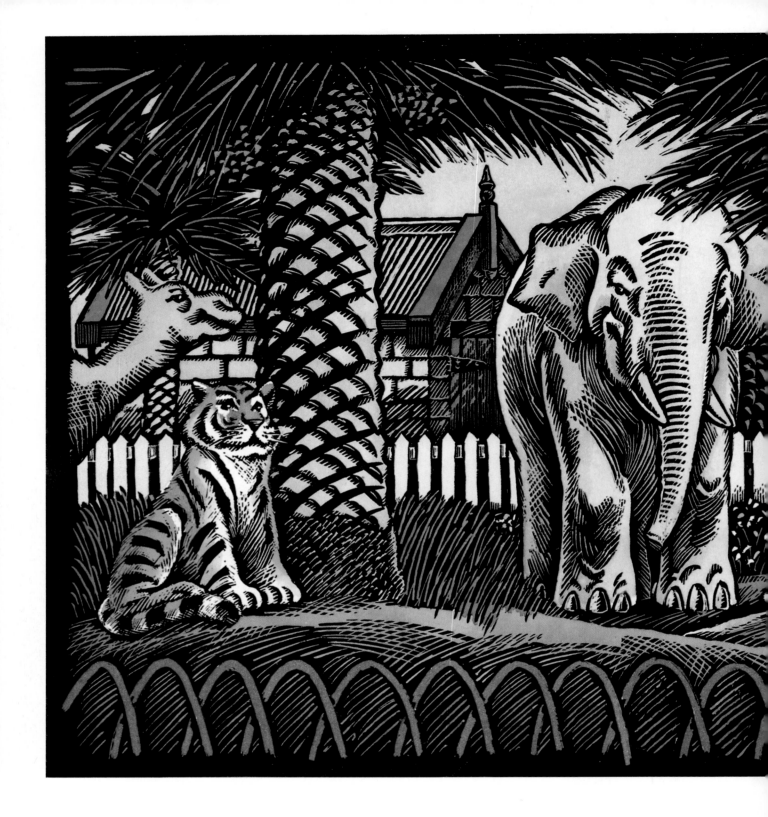

George's family went into the zoo. "This is a very heavy picnic basket," they said. But they didn't open it. George pushed his nose through the lid.

He smelled lions and tigers, and elephants and camels, and bears and giraffes, and emus and ostriches.

George liked the zoo.

His family walked and walked all over
the zoo. Finally, they sat down. They
opened the picnic basket.

"Oh, George!" they said. "Bad dog,
George!"

They were just about to shut the lid,
when—men began to shout, women began
to scream, and the children began to run.

George jumped out of the picnic basket.
There was the biggest cat he had ever seen.
And the cat had the biggest bone he had
ever seen.

George forgot that he had just eaten the
cold chicken, and the ham, and the rolls, and
half the cake.

George wanted that bone!

George's family sat in a tree and called him. But George wanted that bone.

He growled and barked and snapped at the cat. The cat came closer, and roared back the biggest growl that George had ever heard.

George growled and barked and snapped
again. The cat stopped, and men came
running with trucks and ropes and nets, and
chased it into a big cage.

The men locked the cage with a big
lock. The men and the women and the
children stopped screaming. Everyone
looked at George.

George did not want to be chased with trucks and ropes and nets and be locked in a big cage.

He ran back to his picnic basket.

George's family got out of the tree. He
knew that they would say, "Bad dog, George!"
But they didn't. They seemed quite happy.
They said he was a good dog, a wonderful
dog, the bravest, best lion-chasing dog in the
whole world.

Then they picked up the picnic basket
and carried it past the sign that said,
"No Dogs Allowed," and back to the car.

And when they got home, George took
the lion's bone out of the picnic basket . . .

and buried it in the garden.

A House with a Star Inside

A story retold by Melissa Heckler
Illustrated by Holly Hannon

Once upon a time there was a little boy. Oh, he was maybe six or seven years old. One day he went to his mother and he said, "I'm bored." His mother looked at him and he looked at her, and she said with a twinkle in her eye, "You go outside and see if you can find me a little red, round house with no windows and no doors, a chimney on top, and a star inside."

The boy thought about that. Houses weren't round. A round, red house with no windows, no doors, a chimney on top, and a star inside?

Well, he was out the door quickly. He looked around his neighborhood, but all he saw were square houses and houses with windows and doors. He saw lots of chimneys, but he saw no stars, at least not from the outside, so he went on down the road. He was walking and walking, and he saw a girl. He said to her, "Have you seen a red, round house with no windows, no doors, a chimney on top, and a star inside?"

The girl thought for a minute and then she said, "No, I haven't seen a house like that anywhere. I've seen square houses, and I've seen long houses, and I've seen thin houses, but I've never seen a red, round house. But, you know, my father's a farmer, and maybe he'll know 'cause he's seen lots of things."

So the girl and the boy walked on back to her father's farm, and they walked on into the barn where her father was standing. He paused when he saw the two children. They went right up to him and the little girl said, "Papa, this little boy needs some help."

The boy asked the farmer, "Have you seen a red, round house with no windows, no doors, a chimney on top, and a star inside?"

The farmer said, "Hmmmm. I've seen red barns. I've seen all kinds of differently shaped houses. In fact, I've even seen round barns, but I've never seen a red, round house with no windows, no doors, a chimney on top, and a star inside. But I have an idea. You go on down the road and ask Granny. Granny's likely to be sitting out on her front porch rocking. She's old and she's seen lots of things in her time. Maybe she'll have seen one."

So the boy thanked the farmer and the girl, and he ran on down the road till he came to Granny's house. He opened the gate and he went up the front steps. He stopped right on Granny's front porch. "Granny!" he said.

"Good morning," said Granny. "Good morning," said the boy. "Granny, Granny, I'm looking for a red, round house with no windows, no doors, a chimney on top, and a star inside. Have you ever seen one like that?"

Granny rocked and rocked and rocked, then she said, "I've seen lots of things in my day. I've seen lots of kinds of houses, but I've never seen a red, round house with no windows, no doors, a chimney on top, and a star inside. But I'd sure like to read of an evening in a house with a star inside, so if you find that house, you come back and tell me." Granny rocked some more. "Now I have an idea," she said. "You go out into the road and you go ask the wind, because the wind has seen everything and been everywhere. It think perhaps the wind will tell you."

So the boy thanked Granny. He ran down the steps, ran back out the gate, and he just stood in the middle of the road. He opened his arms wide and he shouted, "WIND! WIND! HAVE YOU SEEN A RED, ROUND HOUSE WITH NO WINDOWS, NO DOORS, A CHIMNEY ON TOP, AND A STAR INSIDE?"

Then he waited. Pretty soon he felt a little push at his back. Just a little breeze, it was. But as he waited, the breeze picked up. It was just a little wind, but it seemed to be pushing the boy down the road. So he just went on, feeling the wind at his back, and it pushed him right up a hill. When he got to the top of that hill, the wind pushed him just a little farther, until he was standing right beneath a tree. He looked up at the tree. He saw its leaves.

Through the leaves he saw one other thing. It was an apple. Just then, the wind came, and it blew that apple right off the tree so it fell down at the boy's feet. The boy picked up the apple, and he looked at it. It was red and round. It had no windows, no door, and a chimney on top. But where was the star?

The boy didn't wait more than ten seconds. He ran off down the road. He ran past Granny's house and he yelled, "Granny, I think I've found it. I'll come back and show you!"

He ran on to his mother. He ran through the front door of his house and he called, "Mama! Mama! I think I've found it!"

His mother came. When she saw he had an apple, she got out a knife and sat down at the kitchen table. She lay the apple on its side and carefully cut it in half. There, right in the center of each half, was a beautiful five-pointed star!

Well, the boy did go back to Granny, and he went back to the farmer and to the girl, too. He showed them all what he had found: a red, round house with no windows, no doors, a chimney on top, and a star inside.

Remember

Written by Pamela Mordecai
Illustrated by Jan Davey Ellis

Remember when
the world was tall
and you were small
and legs were all
you saw?

Thin legs
fat legs
dog legs
cat legs.

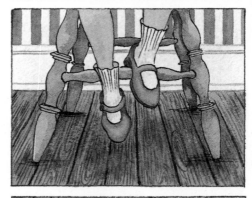

Table legs
chair legs
dark legs
fair legs.

Quick legs
slow legs
nowhere-
to-go legs.

Jumping legs
prancing legs
skipping legs
dancing legs.

Shoes-and-sock legs
on the rocks legs.

Standing-very-tall legs
running-all-around legs.

Stooping-very-small legs
lying-on-the-ground legs.

Remember when
the world was tall
and you were small
and legs were all
you saw?

POP'S TRUCK

Written by Honey Anderson and Bill Reinholtd
Illustrated by Pam Posey

Dan and Wendy liked going to Pop's
house because he lived on a farm.

There were sheep, chickens,
pigs, one cow, and an
old dog to play with at
Pop's farm.

But best of all, there
was Pop's truck.

"Your truck is great,
Pop," Dan always said.

Pop let the children ride in the back of the truck when he fed out hay to the sheep and the cow.

He let them ride in the back of the truck when he went to check the fences.

Once, he let Wendy sit in the back holding a lamb when its mother was sick.

Pop had to bring the ewe and her lamb up to the sheds, to look after them.

Dan had to sit on the ewe to keep her still, while Pop's truck bounced over the dirt road all the way home.

But last week, when Wendy and Dan
went out to stay at Pop's, they found that
something was wrong.

"Hi, Pop! Where's the truck?" asked
Dan.

"Oh, Dan, it's a long, sad story,"
replied Pop. "That truck has been on
the farm as long as Granny and I have.
It's as old as your mom."

"It's a great truck,
Pop," said Dan.

"It *was* a great truck, Dan, but it's had a long life. Last week, it just seemed to get too tired to go any more."

"It probably needs a new battery or something," Dan said.

"Take it to the garage and get Jim to fix it," Wendy suggested.

"I tried that. The trouble is, it's so old that Jim can't get parts to fix it."

"Well, where is it, anyway?" asked Dan.

"It's been taken to the dump."

"What?" yelled Wendy.

"You can't take the truck to the dump. It's part of the family," said Dan. "How would you like to be taken to the dump just because you'd got old and tired?"

"Well, that's where it is," said Pop. "I can't have useless machinery lying around the farm. Come and look at the new truck I bought. It's in the garage."

"I don't even want to see it," said Wendy. "I'd rather go to the dump and see the old truck."

"Yes, so would I," agreed Dan.

"Well, how about a ride in the back of the new truck, down to the dump? You could say good-bye to the old one," suggested Pop.

"O.K."

Wendy and Dan ran to the garage, and there was a very shiny, new blue truck.

"The old truck never had to go in the garage," muttered Dan. "It was tough enough to live outside for thirty years."

"I hate blue trucks," Wendy said to Dan, as she scrambled into the back of the new truck. "And there are no old sacks in the back to sit on."

They sat quietly in the back of the truck,
while Pop drove down the driveway to the gate.
Dan hopped out, opened the gate, and then
closed it after Pop had driven through.

As they drove down the road to the dump,
they noticed that the new truck wasn't
nearly as bumpy to ride in.

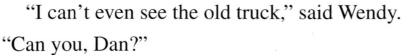

"I can't even see the old truck," said Wendy. "Can you, Dan?"

"No. Oh . . . Oh, yes, I mean. Look, Wendy! There it is. It's just over there, by the storage shed. But why is it up there, instead of down in the valley with all the junk?"

The old truck was parked on the top of the hill, with its cab and engine pointing down into the dump. It seemed to be looking over the whole scene.

As Pop stopped near the old truck, the
children were surprised to see that someone
was sitting in the front.

It was Dave, the man in charge of the dump.
He was having a cup of tea, and he had his
thermos propped up on the seat next to his paper.

"Hello, Bill," he said to Pop. "That truck of yours was just too good to bury with all the garbage. I got the boys to haul it up here for me. It makes a great office. It keeps me warm and dry. It's a great truck."

"There you are, Pop," whispered Dan. "Why didn't you think of that? You could have used it for an office at the farm."

"Well, Dan, you're probably right," replied Pop. "But to tell you the truth, I don't really need an office that badly."

"Well, at least someone can still use it," said Dan. "And it didn't have to be crushed to pieces."

"And," Wendy said to Dave, "you get a really good view from here!"

"What about coming into my office for
a cup of tea?" asked Dave.
"That would be great," said Wendy.
"That would be terrific," said Dan.

Trixie

Written by Rick Brownell
Illustrated by Joy Antonie

I love going to the
dump. There's always
so much to see. The
seagulls must think so,
too, because there are
always millions of them
flying around.

I remember the day I first saw
Trixie. Dad and I had just arrived at
the dump and we were starting to unload
the station wagon. A dog walked up to the car.

"Look, Dad!" I said. "That dog has only
three legs."

"Well, it sure does. Poor thing must have been
hit by a car. It probably had to have that leg taken
off by the vet."

"Dad, can I pet her?"

Dad took a closer look at the three-legged dog and said, "Come here, Girl." He clicked his tongue a couple of times and the three-legged dog came up to him. She seemed a little shy, but her tail was wagging. Dad put his hand out and let the dog sniff it so she would know he wanted to be friendly. The he petted her on the head.

"She seems to be friendly. I think it's O.K. for you to pet her," he said.

As soon as I put out
my hand, the three-legged
dog gave it a big lick. I
think she liked me right
away. I sure liked her!

"Dad, I like this dog and she likes
me. Can I take her home?"

Just as Dad was about to answer,
there was a loud whistle.

"Get over here, Trixie, and stop
bothering those people."

As the man walked toward us, I said, "This dog's not bothering us, Mister. She's a nice dog. Is she yours?"

"Oh, yes. She's mine all right. I've had Trixie since she was a pup. Of course, with one leg missing, she doesn't get around as well as she used to, but she does all right."

Dad finished dumping the trash and said, "Come on, Emma. It's time to go."

"Goodbye, Trixie. See you next time."

From then on,
seeing Trixie was
the best part of
going to the dump.
We discovered that
Gus, Trixie's owner,
worked at the dump and that Trixie
went to work with Gus every day.

I'd always look for Trixie as we pulled into the
dump. I'd jump out of the car as Trixie headed
our way. I knew she was happy to see me
because her tail would be wagging–but not so
hard that it would make her fall down.

I'd give Trixie a big
pet and scratch her above
the tail the way she liked it.
Then I'd throw a stick for her to
fetch while Dad unloaded the car. Trixie
was a good fetcher, but I never threw the
stick too far, because Gus had told me that I
shouldn't make Trixie too tired.

One day, as Gus
wandered over, he said,
"Hi, Emma. I see you're
watching my dog for me again."

"Hello, Gus," I said. "Yes, I'm
taking good care of her. I'm not
throwing the stick too far, though. Gus,
how did Trixie lose her leg?"

"Well, Emma," Gus said, "Trixie always
liked to run out in the woods to chase the
squirrels and just wander around. Once, she
didn't show up after dark, and I began to worry.

"The next morning, I went out
to look for her. I searched all day
long and finally found her, caught
in a trap.

"She'd been lying there all night and
was so weak that she couldn't even lift her
head. So I put her over my shoulders and
carried her home.

"That trap had hurt
her leg pretty badly,
and it was easy to see
that she was in pain.
The vet thought it
would be best to just put
her to sleep. But I couldn't stand the
thought of losing Trixie. She's my best friend.
The vet said that the only way she might live
would be to take her wounded leg off."

"That must have been awful for you, Gus, and
for Trixie," I said.

"Yes, Emma. It was. After the operation she was
a pretty sick pooch. I didn't know if she would ever
be well enough to get up out of her bed.

"Then one day, I was sitting at the kitchen table, and I heard a clippity, clippity, clop sound. I turned around and there was Trixie standing on her three legs, wagging her tail."

"She's really a great dog, Gus."

"Yes. She's my best friend, aren't you, Trixie?" Gus said, as he petted her.

Several weeks later,
Dad and I took another
load of junk to the dump.
As usual, I looked for Trixie,
but she didn't come running up to the car.

"Do you see her, Dad?" I asked.

"No, I don't, Emma. But don't worry, she'll
show up. She always does," Dad said. "Come
on. Help me unload the car."

I kept a look out for
Trixie as I helped unload the car.

"Dad, I can't even see Gus."

"Perhaps Gus and Trixie have
the day off," Dad said. I knew he was
worried, too.

"Perhaps Gus doesn't work here any
more. But we'll drive around to the other
side in case he's working over there."

And there he was–coming out of a shed.
I jumped out of the car and ran up to Gus.

"Gus, where have you been? We've been looking all over for you."

"Well, hello, Emma," Gus said. "I've been kind of busy. You see, I've been playing nurse for Trixie."

"For Trixie? Is she O.K.?" I exclaimed.

"Come and see for yourself," Gus said.

Dad and I followed Gus to the shed. It was dark, so it took a minute before we could see.

"It must have happened early this morning," Gus said, as he pointed to the corner.

And there lay
Trixie—with six little
golden puppies cuddled
up to her.

"Oh, Trixie!" I exclaimed.
Trixie's tail started wagging
as she heard my voice. "Oh, your
babies–they're just beautiful!"

"They sure are!" said Gus. "But in two
months I'm going to have six more dogs than
I know what to do with."

He looked at Dad and then at me and then
back at Dad.

"I wonder how I'm going to find homes for them.
Any ideas about a home for one?" he said, as he
winked at Dad.

"Dad! Gus! I know
someone who needs a
puppy. *I* need one. Really I do!"
    Dad looked down at me with
a smile and said, "I'm sure you do.
And why not!"
    I'm sure Trixie smiled before she shut
her eyes and went to sleep.
    And I'm sure one puppy smiled, too. She's
going to be my puppy soon.

THE THREE WISHES

• An Old Story •

Written and illustrated by Margot Zemach

84

Long ago, a man and his wife lived peacefully at the edge of a great forest. All the year round, they worked together as woodcutters.

Every morning, at sunrise, they went into the forest, where they cut trees and branches into logs. At sunset, they carried them home. But no matter how hard or how long they worked, they often went hungry.

Early one morning, as they were working in the forest, they heard a faint voice calling: "Help, help, someone help me!" The voice seemed to be coming from an old tree that had fallen nearby.

The man and his wife ran to the tree. There on the ground lay a small imp kicking his legs. His tail was caught under the fallen tree! "Help, Help," the imp cried weakly.

"We'll help you gladly," the man and his wife said together. And they pushed and pushed till the tree rolled off.

The imp sprang straight up into the air, joyfully twirling his tail. "A hundred thanks for your kindness," he said. "I have been lying here in misery ever since this tree fell. To thank you for saving me, I will give you three wishes. There are only three, so wish wisely, my friends—and goodbye!" Then he flew up among the branches and disappeared.

The man and his wife were delighted with their good luck. All that cold day, they were warmed by thoughts of the three wishes that would soon be theirs. "We might wish for fine clothes and silver," thought the wife, "or even for a grand house with flower gardens and fruit trees."

In the evening, as they trudged home, the man thought: "We might wish for a donkey to carry this wood, or even a horse and cart to ride in."

"That's so, that's so," he said to himself, and his bundle of wood seemed to grow lighter.

When they got home, the man and his wife settled down to talk about their three wishes. "We might wish for fine clothes and silver," said the wife, "or a grand house with beautiful flower gardens and fruit trees."

"Or we might wish for a donkey to carry the wood, or even a horse and cart to ride in ourselves," said the man.

"Or we might wish for great chests of jewels," said the wife.

"Or even a mountain of gold coins!" said the man.

"We might wish never to go hungry again," said the wife.

"That's so, that's so," said the man. "But just now I wish we had a pan of sausages for our dinner."

No sooner said than done. That very instant, a pan of sausages appeared, sizzling and smoking on the fire.

"Oh, you fool!" said the wife. "Look what you've done! How I wish those sausages were hanging from your big nose!"

No sooner said than done. The sausages leaped from the pan and hung heavily from the man's nose.

"Oh, wife, see what you've done!" he cried. "Who's the fool now?"

93

The man and his wife tried every which way to get the sausages off. But, pull and tug as they might, all their efforts were useless. The sausages remained hanging from the poor man's nose.

Finally, too tired to move, the man and his wife slumped down before the fire.

They thought with longing of their one last wish. Should it be the donkey to carry the wood, the horse and cart to ride in together, the grand house, the fine clothes and jewels, or the mountain of gold coins? Any one of these wishes could still be theirs.

But what would be the good of it if the man must live his whole life with sausages hanging from his nose?

So they joined hands, and with their last wish they wished the sausages OFF.

No sooner said than done! The sausages were back in the pan, sizzling and smoking and smelling delicious.

So the man and his wife sat down cheerfully to a fine dinner.

"Well now, we've not done too badly," said the wife.

"That's so, that's so!" the man agreed.

Tom's Friend

Written and Illustrated
by Pat Reynolds

"Mom! Where are you? Look what I've found!"
Tom came running up to the back door, excited
and out of breath.

"He was by the long grass near the back fence.
Probably lives in the bushes along the creek. He
likes me, Mom. Look, you can tell—he's smiling.
And he didn't run away. I was very gentle with
him. He didn't mind when I picked him up. He
likes me and I want to keep him . . ."

"What have you got there?" asked his mom.

Tom held out the bucket she used to water her plants.

Curled up in the bottom was a big lizard. It didn't fit in the bucket very well, and it looked up at them awkwardly with one bright eye.

"Look at his nose holes," said Tom. He pointed to the bucket, but his hand shot back again when the lizard threw open its mouth and revealed a very blue tongue.

"Why did he do that?" Tom was shocked that his new friend had been unfriendly.

"You frightened him, so he tried to scare you off. That's how he protects himself from dogs and cats and big birds."

193

"Well it's a good trick!" said Tom.

"He must be a bluetongue lizard. I think I'll call him Bluey. He can be my new pet. I'm going to make him a home right now. This bucket is too small." And he rushed off.

"Wait a minute . . ." called Mom.

But Tom didn't hear her, and she went inside with a half-smile, half-frown on her face.

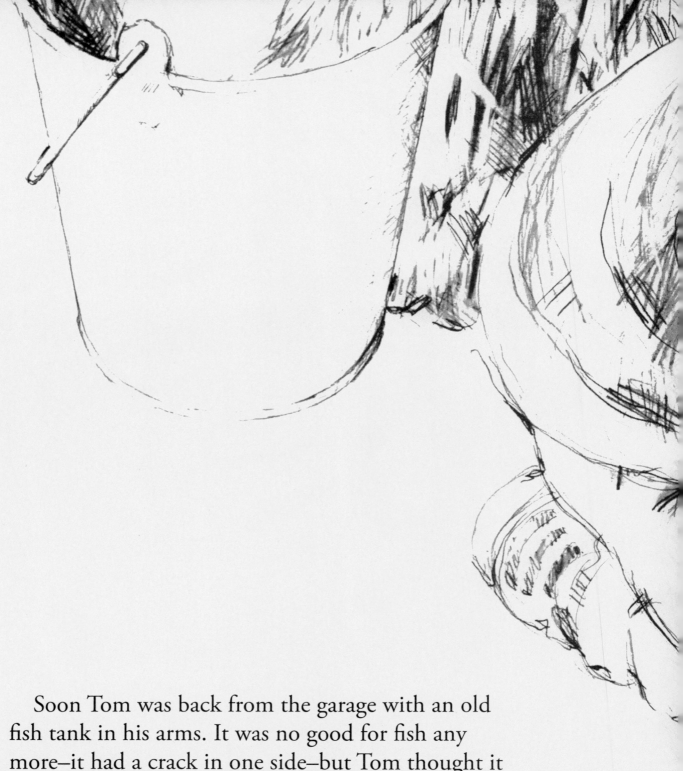

Soon Tom was back from the garage with an old fish tank in his arms. It was no good for fish any more–it had a crack in one side–but Tom thought it might be comfortable for a lizard.

He filled the bottom with sand and rocks. Then he put a dish in one corner, for water, and planted some tufts of grass in the other.

"It's ready, Mom," he called.

He put on one of her gardening gloves, just to be safe, and gently carried the lizard from the bucket to the glass tank.

"There you go, Bluey," he murmured.

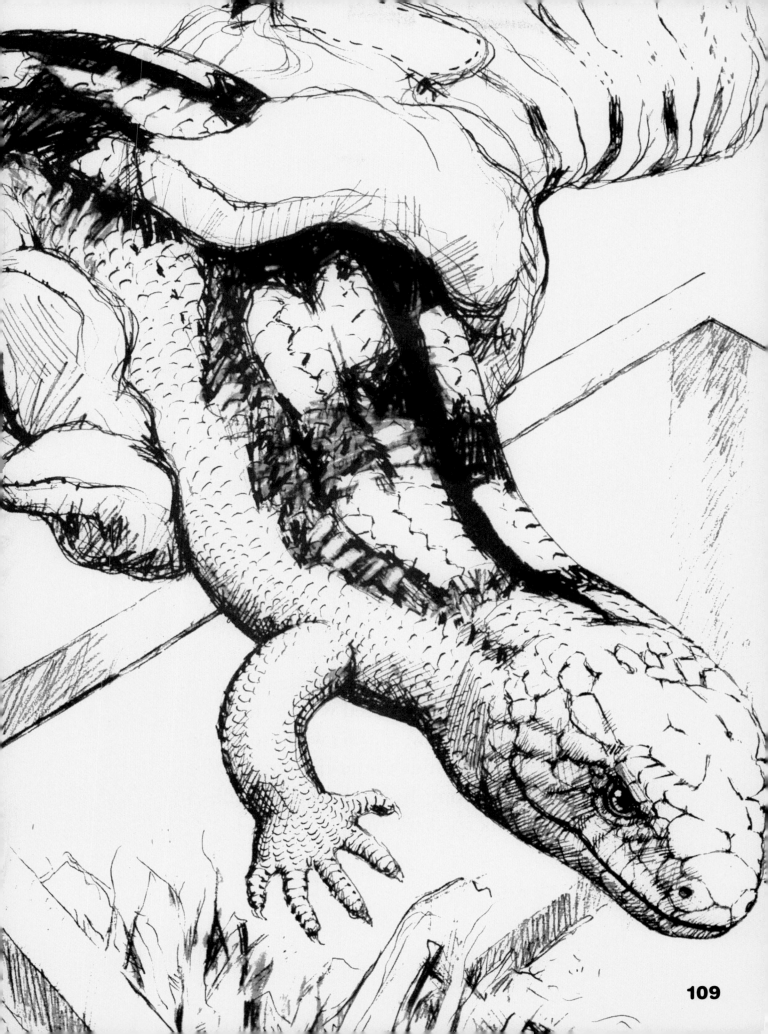

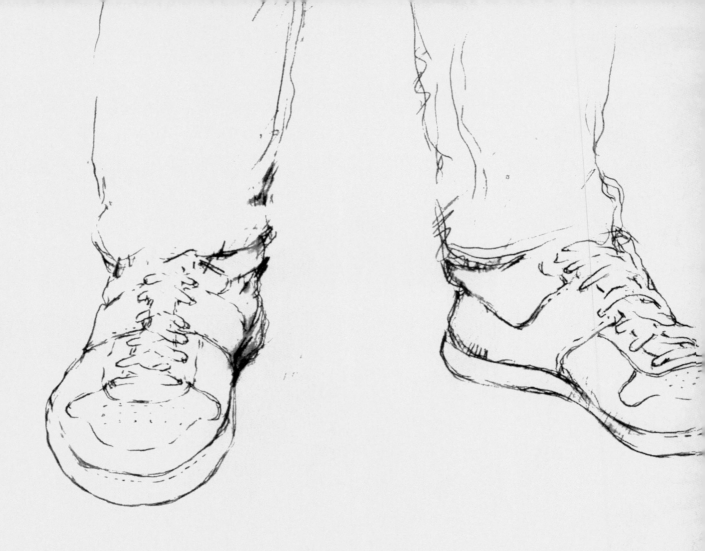

Mom came out to have a look. Tom certainly tried hard to make a good home for the lizard.

"See," he said, very pleased with himself. "He can move around now. He has water to drink, and somewhere to hide under that grass. What do lizards eat, Mom? Insects and things like that?"

"Yes, I think so. And fruit."

"Do you think he would eat hamburger?"

"Probably."

But there was something wrong. Mom didn't look happy.

"Did I forget something?" Tom asked.

"Well, yes and no," said Mom with that half-smile, half-frown.

Tom protested. "He has everything he needs. What have I forgotten?"

"Come with me, Tom."

She held his hand and they walked down to the bottom of the backyard.

"Show me where you found the lizard."

"Here. He was sitting in the sun next to
this long grass."

"Tom," said Mom, "I want you to imagine
that you're a lizard, and tell me what you're
going to do today."

Tom's eyes lit up. "O.K.," he said. "Well, first I'm going to lie in the sun here for awhile. Then I'll creep down there, through the long grass, to the creek for a drink. Then . . . I think I'll catch some fat ants for lunch, over there where they live in the mound. And now I'll stretch out on that big flat rock over there, by the water, and have my after-lunch nap."

"I might go for a walk up the creek after that, to see what's there, since you never let me go that far, and then . . ."

"Let's go back to the house now," said Mom. And they walked back, with Tom pulling her up the hill because she always pretended to be out of breath.

"Can you see what's missing now?"

Tom looked at the lizard in the tank and his face grew sad. He knew what she meant.

"I think I'd better let him go, Mom," he said.

Mom squeezed his hand. "I think Bluey really likes you for that. Look, he's smiling!"

Swap

Written by Carol Diggory Shields
Illustrated by Cynthia Fisher

Mom made me a peanut butter sandwich,
I traded at lunch for a tuna on rye.
Swapped my orange for Jonathan's corn chips,
And traded my cookies for a marshmallow pie.

Traded the chips for a handful of pretzels,
Gave up my milk for a tropical punch.
Changed the tuna for Ben's bologna,
Swapped the pie for the cake in Kim's lunch.

Gave the bologna for a bagel with cream cheese,
Swapped the cake for yummy Gummy Bears.
Sold the punch for a shiny, new quarter,
Traded the pretzels for a nice, ripe pear.

Bought some cold milk with a quarter,
Traded the bears for a pudding cup.
Swapped the bagel for Joe's ham sandwich,
Exchanged the pudding for a Fruit Roll-Up.

Gave the ham for a peanut butter sandwich,
Took an orange for the fruit roll snack.
Swapped the pear for two chocolate-chip cookies…
I think I just got my old lunch back.

The Thirsty Crows

Retold by Faye W. Daggett
Illustrated by David Fischer

Three crows were in the middle of a hot, dry desert. They had gone without eating or drinking for two days, and they were still very far from their home. If they kept on going, it would take them more than a day to reach their home. But they could not keep on going. They were too weary, too hungry, and too thirsty. The youngest crow said, "I can't go on. I'm going to lie down right here and die."

The oldest and wisest crow said, "No, we must try to keep going."

The middle crow said, "But I do not have enough strength to fly."

The oldest crow said, "Then we will walk."

And so they walked. They walked down into a dry valley where there was an old narrow well. The crows used all their strength to hobble over to the well. They could smell fresh water, but when they looked down into the well, their hearts saddened. There was water in the bottom of the well, and the bottom of the well was not very far down, but it was too far for them to reach.

The oldest crow told the others to hang onto his legs, and he would see if he could reach the water with his beak. They lowered him into the narrow well as far as they could, but still, the water was out of reach.

The middle crow said, "We can't fly down to get the water. The well is not wide enough. We can't reach the water unless we fly or jump down there. So we will not find anything to drink here."

The oldest crow said, "We can't go to the water, but we can bring the water to us."

How can we do that?" the youngest crow asked.

The oldest crow explained. "We can pick up pebbles with our beaks and drop them into the well. Each pebble that goes to the bottom makes the bottom a little higher. When the bottom of the well moves up, the water will move up. If we drop enough pebbles, the water will be high enough for us to reach."

The middle crow said, "Your plan sounds crazy to me, but we should try it. We have no choice other than dying out here."

So the three weakened crows picked up pebbles and dropped them one at a time into the well. After they had dropped many, many pebbles, the middle crow looked down into the well and said, "I knew this plan was crazy. It's not working. The water is still beyond our reach."

"Ah," said the oldest crow. "But if you look closely, you'll see that the water is a little higher than it was—a little closer to us."

The youngest crow said, "I can't drop any more pebbles. I'm too weary. I'm going to lie down and die, right here."

"That is a good plan," the oldest crow said. "If you die, we will throw you into the well and your body will raise the level of the water far more than a hundred pebbles would."

"No," the youngest crow said. "I don't want to be thrown into a well, and I don't want to die."

The oldest crow said, "Then help yourself stay alive by dropping pebbles into the well."

The sun burned down, and the crows were so weary that they could hardly move, but they kept working at their task—all day long. And as the sun was finally setting in the west and the sand was finally starting to cool, the three crows each dropped one more pebble into the well and looked at the wonderful cool water. It was very close now. The youngest crow said, "I think I can reach that water with my beak." And he did. He began to drink. The others joined in. They drank their fill and they rested next to the well. They felt stronger and refreshed.

The oldest crow said, "We are still hungry, but soon we will have enough strength to fly home."

"Yes," the middle crow said. "Your plan worked. It saved our lives."

The oldest crow said, "Let this be a lesson to both of you. Every little bit makes a difference. We made a little difference with each pebble we dropped. And those little differences added up to a big difference."

The crows did not die. They flew home the next morning, and each of them lived a long, full life. The middle crow and the youngest crow became very wise because they never forgot the lesson they had learned in the desert.

Rabbit Poem

Written by Pamela Mordecai

Illustrated by Teri Weidner

To keep
a rabbit
is a good
habit.

A rabbit is truly
curious:
his eyes are soft
but his whiskers
wiggle
and his nose twitches
and his ears jiggle

and his tail
is a bump
on
his rump.

A rabbit
is cheerful
but not especially
careful
about multiplying:
the answers
he gets
to the simple
sum
of one and one
are mystifying…

A rabbit is easy
to care for:
to munch on grass
is what he's hare
for…

So if you get
the chance
to have a rabbit,
grab it!

Moonwalker

Written by Carol Diggory Shields
Illustrated by Jan Davey Ellis

I'm a moonwalker, walking on the moon.
I'm a jungle stalker, stalking wild baboons.
I'm a superhero, skimming through the blue.
Puddle jumping, leaf-pile leaping, I'm a kangaroo.

I'm a desert rattlesnake, sliding through the sand.
Counting out the beat, I'm the leader of the band.
I'm Tyrannosaurus, looking for a snack.
Whoo-whoo! I'm a train, rolling down the track.

I'm a red-eyed robot, clanking up the road.
I'm an eighteen-wheeler with a heavy load.
I'm a famous rock star, moving very cool.
Actually,
    I'm just me,
        Walking home from school.

See the Rabbits

Part 1
Written by Harvey Cleaver
Illustrated by Ted Tadiello

One day a few years ago, when I was six years old, my parents told me, "This weekend, we're going to see the rabbits in Iowa."

I was standing next to my older brother Gordey. We had just come home from school.

Gordey said, "Isn't that where Aunt Jen and Uncle Dick live?"

"That's right," Dad said. "Do you remember the last time we went there?"

"Sure," Gordey said. "It was just after we got the blue Ford. I remember it broke down when we were in Iowa, and we spent a whole day in the garage, waiting for it to get fixed."

"Yes," Mom said. "That part of the visit was not too much fun." Then Mom turned to me and asked, "Do you remember the trip, Dennis?"

"I . . . I . . ." I didn't remember one thing. I'd heard the names Dick and Jen, but I didn't have memories of any faces to go with the names.

"Well" Dad said to me, "you were less than three years old the last time we visited them. So you probably had other things to think about."

Gordey said, "Either that or he forgot to wind up his mind that weekend."

"Not funny," I said to Gordey and made my best sour face at him, but he was already making his goofy face at me and saying, "Gee, I don't remember anything. I was just a little baby."

"Well, I can't help it," I said.

It was Wednesday and we were going to leave on Saturday morning, very early. That meant I had to get ready for a long car trip. I always had two kinds of problems on these trips. The first problem was trying to sit in a car hour after hour without going nuts. The other problem was Gordey. He would always do something to get me mad. Then we'd argue until Mom and Dad would make us stop.

This time, it would be different. I'd bring along all kinds of things so I wouldn't get bored–paper, crayons, books, games. And then if Mom and Dad would just let me sit in the front seat by the window, Gordey wouldn't be able to start anything.

Before we left on the trip, Dad took out a map and showed everybody the road we would take. Dad touched the town where we lived in Illinois and said, "We're going to take this road to Iowa, and all the way to see the rabbits." He traced a red line with his finger. When he stopped, he said, "It's going to take us more than five hours, so Gordey and Dennis, I want you to relax and be patient."

I wanted to be patient, but I didn't know how long five hours felt.

Even before we left, I was getting impatient. After we were already sitting in the car with all our stuff, Mom said that we had to go to the bathroom before we left. I told her that I didn't have to go, but she insisted.

I didn't get to sit in the front seat by the window. Mom did. I could have sat in the middle of the front seat, but that's the worst seat in the whole car. You don't even have your own window. So I sat in the back with you-know-who. Before we were a block from home, he started to mess with the paper I had brought along. "That's mine," I explained. "If you want paper, bring your own."

"Now, now," Mom said. "There's enough paper for both of you. I'm sure you won't mind sharing with your brother." Mind? I hated it.

"Why can't he bring his own things?" I asked. "Why does he always have to . . ."

"Settle down," Dad said.

Just then, I saw two kids that we played with–Eddie and Amy. I rolled my window down, waved at them, and announced, "We're on our way to see the rabbits in Iowa." I had to talk very fast because we were moving at 30 miles an hour.

Mom thought it would be fun to play license-plate games. So first we played a color game. You'd get a point if you saw a red license plate. The Illinois plates were white, and that's what most of the cars had. The game was boring because we went for a long time before anybody spotted a red plate. Then guess who saw three of them and won the game? Gordey. I saw only one.

So we played another license-plate game. Dad said, "Let's see who gets the most license plates that start with the number nine." That was more fun than the red game. Mom won this game. I came in last, of course.

Then we played the out-of-state license game. You'd get a point for every out-of-state plate you spotted. Mom and Gordey tied in this game. By now, I was really tired of license-plate games. So I decided to draw some pictures. Mom said, "Why don't you draw a picture of the family?"

That was a good idea. I had drawn a large picture of the family in school, and everybody there thought it was great. I was working with smaller paper than I had in school, but I was being very careful. When I was done, my picture had a nice blue sky on top and green grass along the bottom. Dad and Mom were in the middle. I was next to Dad. Gordey was next to Mom.

I was wearing my big hiking boots and my thick belt. Dad was wearing a big cowboy hat. Everybody in the family had their arms out to the side, and we were smiling. Gordey's smile looked a little funny. I think the car went over some bumps when I was drawing him. So his lips were big and sort of crooked.

I told everybody, "I'm done."

"Let's see," Mom said. I handed her the picture. "Very nice," she said. "I see that you're wearing your new hiking boots."

Dad said to her, "Oh, is that supposed to be Dennis? He's bigger than Gordey."

"Let me see that picture," Gordey said. Mom held it up, and Gordey started to go on and on about what a bad picture it was. He laughed, "Hee haw, hee haw." Then he said, "So that little thing on the end is suppose to be me? I'm glad you didn't draw the dog in this picture because she probably would have been bigger than me, too. What a terrible looking picture."

"It's a nice picture," Mom said. "It's not that easy to draw things the size you want."

"Sure," Gordey said as he looked right at me. "I can't draw things the size I want so I'm going to draw myself really big, and I'll draw my big brother about half as big as I am."

Dad said, "Listen to this." Then he started to sing, "Row, row, row your boat, gently down the stream . . ."

We all joined in. We sang the song about ten times. Then Mom started singing, "She'll be comin' round the mountain when she comes . . ."

And we sang that song for a while. Then we sang "On top of old Smoky," "Someone's in the kitchen with Dinah," and some songs I had never sung before like "Don't sit under the apple tree with anyone else but me . . ."

We sang and sang until singing was no longer any fun. Then I had to go to the bathroom. "Already?" Dad said. "Didn't you go before we left?"

"Yes, I did, but I still have to go."

So we stopped at a gas station. Then we drove some more. I drew two more pictures, but I didn't show them to anyone. One of them was a picture of Gordey and our dog, Stubby. Stubby was way bigger than Gordey. Ha, ha.

See the Rabbits

Part 2
Written by Harvey Cleaver
Illustrated by Ted Tadiello

We went down the highway a long time, and I watched a lot of telephone poles go by. I began to wonder how close we were to seeing the rabbits. Maybe we were almost there. The only way to find out was to ask. "Are we almost there?"

Dad said, "No, Dennis. We've only been on the road for about an hour and a half."

"Really? What time is it now?"

"It's about nine. We won't be there until long after we've eaten lunch."

We ate lunch on a bench at a rest stop. It was windy and my glass of orange drink blew over. Also, when I was eating my egg-salad sandwich, a big glop slid out and landed on my shirt and pants. I tried to wipe it away, but it just got messier and uglier.

"Dennis, Dennis," Mom said. "Let's see if I can clean that off." She got some wet paper towels and scrubbed the goop off, but she left a big wet stain. Gordey started laughing. Then mom laughed, too. When I looked at myself I laughed. I did look pretty bad.

To keep from going nuts during the rest of the trip, I thought about the rabbits we were going to see. I liked rabbits. Eddie once had a pet rabbit, and it was really big and neat. You could pet it and everything. I hoped we'd see some of those great big rabbits.

It felt like we had been driving for at least five hours, so I asked dad, "How much longer before we get there?"

"Still a couple of hours," he said.

I waited a long, long time before I asked again. "Are we almost there yet?"

Mom said, "Don't ask those questions any more, Dennis. We'll be there when we get there."

Much, much later, we came to the edge of a large city. Dad turn around and said, "Well, folks, here we are. See the rabbits."

Everybody else said, "Yea."

I said, "Where are they?"

"Where are what?" Dad asked.

"The rabbits."

"What rabbits?"

"You said, 'see the rabbits.'"

Everybody was quiet for a little bit. Then Dad started to laugh. "Oh no," he said. "Not see the rabbits. Cedar Rapids. We're in Cedar Rapids, Iowa."

The others laughed. I didn't. I said, "Do you mean we're not going to see the rabbits? I thought that's why we were going here."

Gordey said, "You thought we were going
to see rabbits? That's great. I can't wait to tell
Eddie and the others. See the rabbits."

Ho, ho. Everybody else thought that was
such a good joke. But I had really been
looking forward to seeing those rabbits.
And now . . . what a wasted trip.

When we finally got to Dick and Jen's place, they said all those things that relatives say. "My, my, how you've grown. Why, I never would have recognized Dennis. He's quite a young man." Then I had to kiss them. I didn't remember them at all, but they seemed nice.

They had fruit and nuts and other treats. I was eating some of those curved nuts while everybody else went into the kitchen. I could hear Dad telling them something in the kind of voice he uses when he's trying to keep a secret. Then everybody laughed. "See the rabbits?" Dick shouted, and I had a pretty good idea what Dad had told them. "That's amazing," Dick said. "That boy must be a genius."

I got up and walked into the kitchen.

I wanted to know why I was a genius.

Both Dick and Jen looked very surprised.

Jen said, "Dennis seemed to know what he was going to see."

"What do you mean?" Mom asked.

Jen said, "Just last week, Dick and I decided what to do with the money we got from selling the store. We decided to buy a rabbit ranch. We are now in the business of raising pedigree rabbits. That's one of the things we wanted you to see–all our beautiful rabbits."

"Wow," I said. "Do you have big ones?"

"We've got some of the very biggest rabbits you have ever seen."

"This is amazing, " Dad said. And he was right.

After supper, we went to the rabbit ranch, and we saw more rabbits than I had ever seen in my whole life. We saw spotted rabbits and black rabbits and white ones with pink eyes and white ones with blue eyes. We saw rabbits that were as big as our dog Stubby, and baby rabbits that were so small they could curl up in my hand. And we got to play with them. Were they ever a lot of fun.

And the next morning, Gordey and I got to go back there and feed them carrots and cabbage and clover. It was great. And that afternoon, when we were getting ready to go back home, guess what Dick and Jen gave us. I'll give you a hint. It was black and white, and it was in a big cage.

We didn't have a name for our rabbit at that time, but later we name her Clover because she really loves clover.

And when we got back home, I was the one who told the story about see-the-rabbits to Eddie and the others. I reminded Eddie, "Remember, I told you we were going to see the rabbits." Everybody thought I was pretty cool.

And when I got back to school, I drew one of my best pictures. It had me and Clover and Stubby and Gordey in it. And guess who was the smallest one in the whole picture. Gordey.

the **Proud**crow

Adapted by Fran Lehr from a fable by Aesop
Illustrated by Joel Snyder

CHARACTERS

NARRATOR
MISS CROW
MR. FOX
3 STALL KEEPERS
TOWNSPEOPLE

SCENE 1

Time:
Once upon a time.

Setting:
A marketplace, with three stalls, one
displaying a pile of vegetables, one
displaying strings of sausage, and one
displaying balls and slices of cheese. TOWNSPEOPLE,
most with baskets on their arms, bustle from stall to stall.
At each stall, a STALL KEEPER stands. All are shouting
loudly—and at the same time:

STALL KEEPER 1:
(Holding high several vegetables)

> Fresh vegetables! Get your fresh vegetables here! Freshest
> in town! Only a few pennies a pound!

STALL KEEPER 2:
(Holding a long string of sausages)

> Sausages! Juicy sausages! Get your sausages here!

STALL KEEPER 3:
(Holding up large pieces of cheese in each hand)

> Yummy cheeses! I've got big cheese and little cheeses!
> Blue cheese and yellow cheese and orange cheese and red
> cheese!

The TOWNSPEOPLE start to buy from the STALL KEEPERS, and the shouting stops. From
stage right, NARRATOR enters and stands near the front of the stage.

153

NARRATOR:

> Once upon a time, in a small village in a far away place, there lived a large, silly crow.

(MISS CROW enters at the back of the stage.)

> Miss crow was very proud. She was proud of her shiny black feathers.

(MISS CROW smiles and pats her feathers.)

> She was proud of her dainty beak.

(MISS CROW rubs her beak.)

> She was proud of her bright, shining eyes.

(MISS CROW flutters her eyes.)

> But most of all, Miss Crow was proud of her singing voice.

(MISS CROW lifts her head, closes her eyes, and opens her beak very, very wide.)

MISS CROW:

> CAW–W–W–W–W!

(Townspeople AND Stall Keepers all cover their ears with their hands and moan MISS CROW is so pleased with her singing that she does not see them. She smiles and bows.

MISS CROW:

> Thank you, thank you! Shall I sing more?

TOWNSPEOPLE and STALL KEEPERS:

> NO!!!

NARRATOR:

You see, Miss Crow's parents were proud of her, too. From the time she was a baby crow, they had told her that she had the best voice of any crow in the country. Which might be true. But you and I know that crows are not songbirds. They make an awful racket. And it's probably true that Miss Crow made the loudest racket of all!

MISS CROW:
(Strutting through the marketplace)

I'm hungry.

(She stops beside the vegetable stall.)

Tomatoes, onions, cabbage. Ugh. Surely there is something here that tastes better.

(She stops beside the sausage stall.)

Sausages might be good, but I did have three sausages for breakfast.

(She stops at the cheese stall.)

Ah, cheese! Now, this is just the food for a crow as special as I am.

STALL KEEPER 3:
(Smiling at a possible customer)

May I help you, Miss Crow? I have quite a selection of wonderful cheeses today.

MISS CROW:
(Frowning, as she looks carefully at each piece of cheese)

Oh, I'm not sure any of these will do for me. They are so common. I need the very best cheese to keep my beautiful feathers shiny, my dainty beak sharp, my black eyes bright. And, of course, my lovely voice lovely.

NARRATOR:

The Stall Keeper is upset that Miss Crow has insulted his cheese. But he is even more upset at the idea of not making a sale.

STALL KEEPER 3:

Although all of my cheeses are excellent, Miss Crow. Indeed, they are the very best in the country.

(He reaches under the counter of his stall and pulls out a tray that contains several large pieces of cheese.)

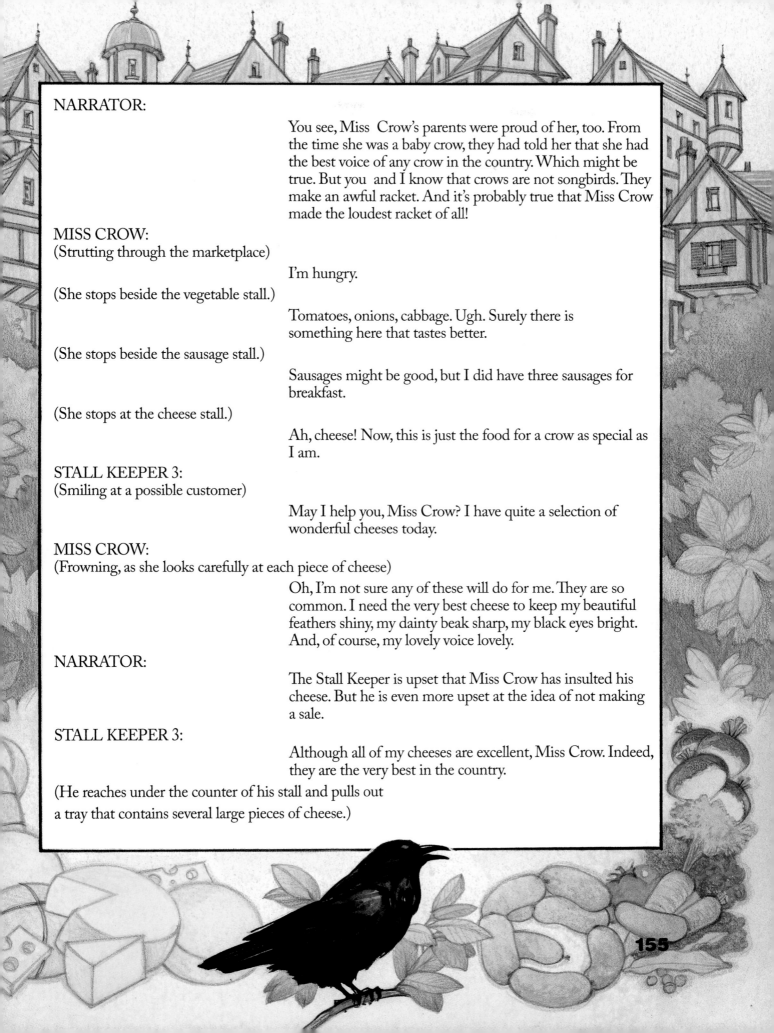

I do have a few cheeses that are so excellent and so rare that I keep them only for my special customers–the ones with the finest tastes. I warn you, though, that they cost much, much more than my other cheeses.

MISS CROW:
(Bending over the tray to examine the cheeses)

Humph! What does cost matter to me? Yes, these cheeses are more to my liking.

(Slowly, as she looks closer at each piece of cheese)

I . . . think . . . I'll . . . have . . . this . . . one!

(She takes the largest piece of cheese in her beak
and skips away through the TOWNSPEOPLE.)

STALL KEEPER 3:
(Running after MISS CROW)

Hey, you didn't pay for that cheese! Bring it back! Come back, you thief! THAT CHEESE IS MINE!

MISS CROW:
(Spreading her wings, ready to fly away)

Silly man! As you can see, the cheese is MINE. For I am not just a pretty bird with an excellent singing voice, I am also a smart bird. And now I'm going off to make a tasty lunch of MY fine piece of cheese. Bye-bye!

(Exits)

SCENE 2

Time:
A few minutes later.
Setting:
A forest. At the center of the stage is a tree, with a large branch—just out of reach from the ground beneath. MISS CROW is settling herself on the branch. She has the large piece of cheese in her beak. NARRATOR enters stage right and stands down stage.

NARRATOR:

Miss Crow is now more proud of herself than ever. She has taken one of the Stall Keeper's best pieces of cheese. Now she is back in the forest, ready to enjoy her stolen lunch. But, wait. Who is this?

(MR. FOX enters, slinking from stage left. He sees MISS CROW, but she does not see him.)

156

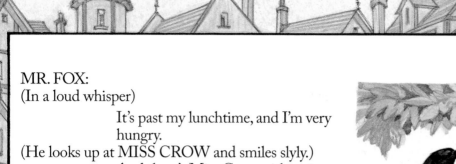

MR. FOX:
(In a loud whisper)

>It's past my lunchtime, and I'm very hungry.

(He looks up at MISS CROW and smiles slyly.)

>And there's Miss Crow with a piece of excellent cheese. Too excellent for a silly crow, but perfect for a clever fox such as I. Now, how can I get it away from her?

(He frowns a bit, thinking.)

>I can't climb the tree and grab it,

(He frowns deeper.)

>because I can't climb trees.

(Thinking harder)

>I can't throw a rock and knock it from her beak,

(Looking around and frowning)

>because there are no rocks and I can't throw.

(His face brightens.)

>I'll have to make her drop it. And I know just the trick to do it!

(He slinks beneath the tree and calls sweetly)

>Good day to you, Miss Crow. I hope you won't mind if I stop to tell you how splendid you look today?

MISS CROW:
(Fluffing out her feathers and sitting taller on the branch)

>Not at all, Mr. Fox. I think I'm looking rather grand myself.

MR. FOX:

>Oh, more than grand–if you don't mind me saying so–more than grand. Your feathers are especially shiny today! Your beak is especially dainty. Your eyes are especially bright–like jewels!

MISS CROW:
(Sitting even taller)

>Yes, yes. That's all true.

MR. FOX:

And from what everyone says, your voice is more beautiful than your feathers; daintier than your beak; lovelier than your eyes. I don't suppose you would be willing to let me hear you sing? Perhaps one little song?

(Turning to the audience and winking)

MISS CROW:

(So taken in by the flattery that she can barely sit still on the branch)

Well, it is my lunchtime. But I suppose I can manage one little song.

(She throws back her head and opens her beak wide.)

CAW–W–W–W–W!

(The piece of cheese falls to the ground, right in front of MR. FOX.)

MR. FOX:

(Grabbing the cheese)

Thank you, Miss Crow! For giving me this excellent cheese, I will give you an excellent piece of advice: Never believe flattery!

(He skips off, eating the cheese.)
NARRATOR:

So Miss Crow learned a very important lesson: Too much pride can make you look like a fool.

(Exits)
MISS CROW:
(Sits on the tree branch, looking sad–and hungry.)

The Fox and the Crow

Retold by Faye W. Daggett

Illustrated by Pat Lucas-Morris

All the other animals knew that the crow was smart. They also knew that the fox was smart. They could not decide who was smarter until the winter of the great snow. During that winter, there was very little food. All the animals were hungry. One cold day, the fox came to visit the crow. They did not like each other, and they did not trust each other. The crow wondered why the fox came to visit her.

The fox said, "Well, I am here because I recognize that you are probably the smartest animal there is."

The crow did not say anything, but the fox's remarks did make her feel good. She said, "Now do not try to flatter me. Tell me why you are here."

The fox said, "I know where there is some delicious cheese, but there is great danger in trying to get it. It is guarded by a dog that does not sleep, and it is in a place that is very hard to reach."

"Tell me more," the crow said.

The fox continued, "If I tell you where the cheese is, you must promise not to tell anyone else about it. We must agree that you and I will be the only ones who share that cheese."

The crow agreed. The fox looked around to make sure nobody else was listening. Then he said, "The cheese is hanging near the top of the cheese maker's barn. Two large pieces are there—one for you and one for me. The problem is getting the cheese. It is guarded by a dog, and it is too high to reach from the floor. So I don't know how we will be able to reach it or get past that terrible dog."

The crow said, "This problem is easy to solve. You go to the front door of the barn and make some noise. The dog will come to chase you away. While the dog is busy with you, I will fly into the barn and snatch the cheese away."

"My, my," the fox said. "You are so very smart. I never would have been able to figure out how to do that. I forgot that you were a bird, and you could fly to high places." Of course, the fox was lying. He knew exactly how to get the cheese, and he said these things to the crow so she would drop her guard and trust him.

The next day the fox and crow carried out their plan. The fox went near the door of the barn and scratched on the wall. The dog barked and charged outside to chase the fox away. The fox could easily outrun the dog, and as he did so, he insulted the dog so it would keep chasing him. "Why don't you stop running?" he shouted to the dog. "You're so slow that you could never catch me."

As the fox kept the dog busy, the crow flew into the barn and grabbed one piece of cheese and dropped it below a nearby chestnut tree. Then the crow flew back and snatched the other piece of cheese in her beak. She kept it there. "This is my piece of cheese," she said to herself, "and that nasty fox will not steal it from me."

After the dog gave up trying to catch the fox and went back to the barn, the fox trotted over to the chestnut tree. "Ah," he said to the crow as he looked at the cheese, "you were able to find the cheese and carry it away. How smart and strong you are. That's a very large piece of cheese. It would take a strong crow to fly with it in her mouth."

The crow did not say anything, but the fox's remarks did make her feel good.

The fox quickly gobbled down his piece of cheese. He licked his chops and said, "Do you know that your voice is nicer than that of any other crow around here?"

"Oh, stop your flattery," the crow said, trying to talk without dropping her piece of cheese.

The fox said, "I'm sure you know that your feathers are much prettier than those on other crows and that your eyes are brighter. But I'm not sure you know that your voice is so much better."

"Oh, stop it," she said, still holding onto her big piece of cheese.

"Please, let me hear you sing," the fox pleaded "Just a little song."

The crow felt very pretty and very smart. She said, "Oh, all right." Then she started to sing. But as soon as she opened her mouth wide enough to sing, the cheese fell from her mouth.

And as soon as the cheese landed on the ground, the fox gobbled it up. He licked his chops and said, "Thank you for the song and for the cheese." And with that he trotted off to tell everybody how he showed that he was the smartest animal in the whole land.

166

The Magic Teakettle

Retold Harriet Winfield

Illustrated by Pat Lucas-Morris

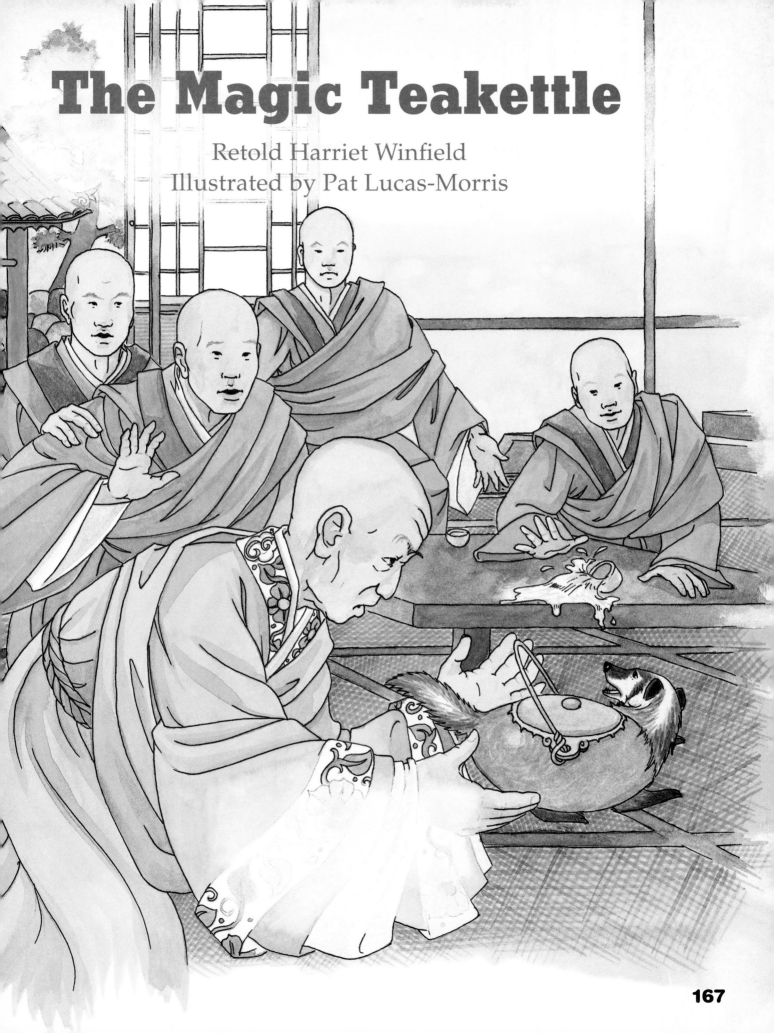

L ong ago in Japan, there was a priest who served tea to his students every afternoon. One day when the priest was shopping, he saw a very interesting iron teakettle. It was rusty and dull, but the priest liked its shape. He said to himself, "This will make a fine kettle for boiling water." He bought the kettle and took it home.

There he polished the old kettle until it looked very handsome. When his students arrived, he showed them the kettle. Then he filled the kettle with water and placed it above the fire.

Moments after the kettle was in place, it started to squeal and squirm. Suddenly, four little badger legs appeared. Then out came a badger head from one end and a badger tail from the other end. "Owwwwww," cried the kettle. "I'm burning up." The kettle started to run around the room.

The priest warned his students, "Don't let that kettle get away." They chased the kettle around and around. Soon the kettle stopped. The little legs went inside, and so did the head and the tail. Once more the kettle was a kettle, not a badger.

The priest was frightened by the kettle. He thought that there was a bad spirit inside. So the next day, when a junkman came by, the priest handed the kettle to him and said, "Give me whatever this kettle is worth." The junkman gave the priest a few pennies and rode off with the kettle.

That night, as the junkman was getting ready to go to bed, he heard a voice calling, "Oh, Mr. Junkman. Oh, Mr. Junkman."

The junkman lit a candle and looked around the room. There was the kettle next to his bed. It was looking at the junkman with its little badger eyes and standing on its four little badger feet. The junkman did not know what to say. "What kind of spirit are you?" he asked.

The kettle said, "I am a good luck spirit. My name is Bumbuku, which means good luck. And if you are good to me, I will bring you good luck."

The junkman said, "I don't see how a kettle can bring me good luck."

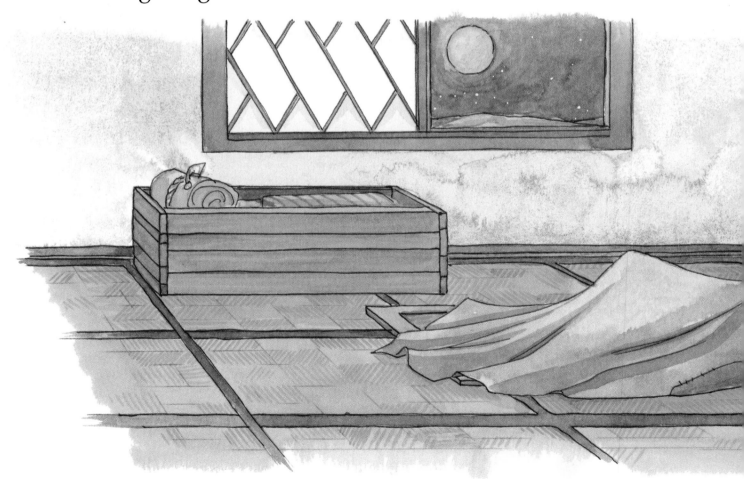

"I can do amazing tricks," Bumbuku said. "If you give me a quiet place to stay and feed me rice cakes every day, I will put on a show. People will come from all over to see my tricks. You will make a fortune."

The junkman thought about what Bumbuku had said. Then the junkman replied, "All right. I will do it. I will give you a quiet place and feed you every day."

"And you must promise to do one more thing," Bumbuku said. "You must never put me near a fire. A priest had me before you did, and he almost burned me to a crisp by putting me near a fire. You must never use me for making tea."

The junkman agreed. The next day, he built a little
theater on one side of his junk yard. He put up a sign
that said "Bumbuku and His Amazing Tricks."

A few people came to see the first show that
Bumbuku put on. The people cheered when they saw his
tricks. He walked across a tightrope holding a parasol in
one hand and a fan in the other. Then he turned into a
kettle. Then he started to spin like a top. He spun and
whirled around and ran into an iron pole. The pole made
a shower of colored sparks, and the people cheered.
Then Bumbuku opened his kettle top and out flew six
white birds. The people clapped and cheered.

Bumbuku put on three shows a day, and by the second day, every seat was filled for every show. People lined up for hours to see Bumbuku's amazing tricks. After two weeks had passed, the little theater was too small to hold all the people who wanted to see him. The junkman raised the price of the tickets again and again, but still the theater was filled for every show that Bumbuku put on.

Finally, the junkman built a large hall that could hold hundreds of people. But the hall was filled for every show. Within a few months, the junkman was very, very rich. He was the richest man in the whole land. And he became richer every day.

After Bumbuku had worked every day for a year, the junkman noticed that Bumbuku seemed tired. The junkman said, "You have worked too hard for me. I have all the money I will ever need, but still you work."

Bumbuku said, "Yes, I am getting tired. I would like to rest as a kettle. I can rest for years if nobody bothers me."

"Well then," the junkman said. "I will take you to a place where you can rest for as long as you wish."

"What place is that?" Bumbuku asked.

"The temple where the old priest lives."

Bumbuku said, "That would be a nice quiet place, but the last time I was there, the priest almost burned me to death. He believes that I am an evil spirit."

The junkman said, "I am sure that you are so famous that he knows of you as the magic teakettle who does amazing tricks and entertains thousands of people. I'm sure the priest would be proud to have you rest in the temple."

The next morning, the junkman took Bumbuku to the temple. The junkman also took lots of Bumbuku's favorite rice cakes and six bags of gold, worth a fortune. At the temple, the junkman explained what Bumbuku wanted to do and why he feared coming back to the temple. The junkman gave all the gold to the priest and asked him if he could find a quiet place where Bumbuku could rest and eat his favorite rice cakes.

The priest said, "Yes, yes. I would be proud to have Bumbuku rest here. I know that he is a kettle of good luck, and I know that he must never be put near a fire. I will make sure that nobody disturbs him for as long as he wants to stay here."

So the priest called his students. They put
Bumbuku on one stand and his rice cakes on another
stand. Then they set these stands up in the treasure
room of the temple, with the rice cakes next to
Bumbuku.

Many people believe that Bumbuku is still in the treasure room of the temple, where he is well taken care of. Every day, the students feed him his favorite rice cakes, and then they let him rest in peace. They never put him near a fire, and he brings the temple good luck.